That You May Have
Life

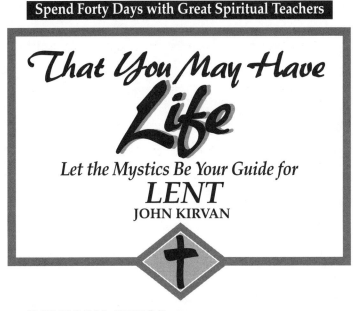

Spend Forty Days with Great Spiritual Teachers

That You May Have *Life*

Let the Mystics Be Your Guide for
LENT
JOHN KIRVAN

AVE MARIA PRESS Notre Dame, Indiana 46556

John Kirvan is the editor and author of several books including *God Hunger* and *Raw Faith* (Sorin Books), and currently lives in Southern California where he writes primarily about classical spirituality.

This work draws on a variety of original sources that have been freely adapted into modern English and rearranged and paraphrased to meet the needs of a meditational format. The passages drawn from Julian of Norwich and Meister Eckhart are based on adaptations made by Richard Chilson, C.S.P., for this series. The passage of John Chrysostom is taken from an English translation by Thomas Halton.

International Standard Book Number: 0-87793-638-2
Cover and text design by Elizabeth J. French.
Printed and bound in the United States of America.

Kirvan, John J.
       That you may have life : let the mystics be your guide for Lent / John Kirvan.
               p.   cm. -- (Thirty days with a great spiritual teacher)
       ISBN 0-87793-638-2
       1. Lent--Meditations. 2. Holy Week--Meditations. 3. Devotional calendars. I. Title. II. Series: 30 days with a great spiritual teacher.
BV85.K48 1998
242'.34--dc21
97-41424
CIP

Contents

I have come that you might have life
and have it more abundantly.

JOHN 10:10

Lent is not only a reminder,
but a continual summons.

JOHN PAUL II

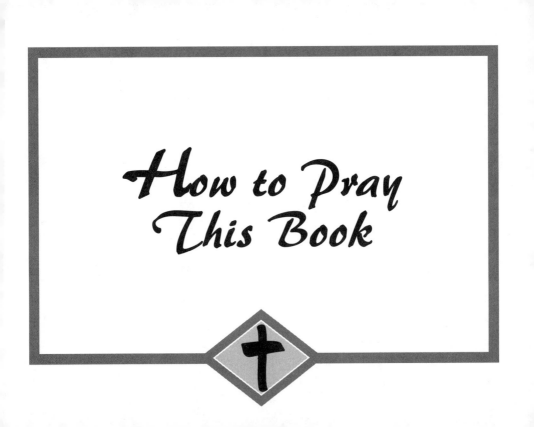

How to Pray This Book

The purpose of this book is to open a new gateway into one of the great spiritual traditions of western Christianity, the observance of Lent, forty days of preparation for celebrating the central mystery of Christianity—the death and resurrection of Jesus. It is a time to contemplate the inescapable connection between new life and our death to what has only seemed like life.

Obviously this is not a book for mere reading. It is a summons to new life. Rather than just engaging us in an act of spiritual and liturgical memory, or inviting us to repeat Lent as a season of familiar routines, this book is designed to take us along a path of meditation and prayer to a life beyond where we are. It is a guide through a series of small deaths blossoming in new life.

That You May Have Life invites us to meditate and pray its words on a daily basis over a period of forty weekdays. Traditionally the Sundays are not counted among Lent's forty days, so we have not included Sunday readings. We suggest that on Sundays you use the scriptural passages assigned by the liturgy.

Just remember that this book is meant to free your spirit, not confine it. If on any day the reading does not resonate well for you, turn elsewhere to find a passage which seems to best fit the spirit of your day and your soul. Don't hesitate to repeat a day as often as you like until you feel that you have discovered what the Spirit, through the words of the author, has to say to your spirit.

To help you along the way, here are some suggestions on one way to use this book as a cornerstone of your daily Lenten prayer. The format employs the three forms of prayer central to the western spiritual tradition: the lesson, the meditation, and the petition. Or if you prefer, reading, reflection, and prayer. So for the forty days beginning on Ash Wednesday and ending on Holy Saturday there is a daily reading for the start of each day selected from the works of the great mystics. There follows a meditation in the form of a mantra to carry with you for reflection throughout the day. And there is a final petitionary prayer for bringing your day to closure.

Over the forty days of Lent you are being invited to dig ever deeper into one of the most profound and joyful of all scriptural promises, that Jesus came that we might have a more abundant life. Each week we are summoned to look for that life beyond the half-lives we lead. Each week we are summoned to the realization that full life lies beyond death, not just death of the body, but the thousand small, daily deaths that must be died if we are to live.

But the forms and suggestions are not meant to become a straitjacket. Go where the Spirit leads you.

As Your Day Begins

As the day begins set aside a quiet moment in a quiet place to do the reading provided for the day.

The passages are short—only two pages long. But they

have been carefully selected to give a spiritual focus, a spiritual
center to your whole day and to carry you day by day into a
deeper understanding of and participation in the Easter
mystery of life beyond death. For each of Lent's six weeks we
have chosen a different spiritual guide, someone whose
experience and wisdom in a special way illuminates the various
deaths that can blossom into more abundant life.

A word of advice: proceed slowly. Very slowly. The
passages have been broken down into sense lines to help you
do just this. Don't read to get to the end, but to savor each
word, each phrase, each image. There is no predicting, no
determining in advance what short phrase, what word will
trigger a response in your spirit. Give God a chance. After all,

you are not reading these passages, you are praying them. You are establishing a mood of spiritual attentiveness for your whole day. What's the rush?

All Through Your Day

Immediately following the day's reading you will find a single sentence, a meditation in the form of a mantra, a word borrowed from the Hindu tradition. This phrase is meant as a companion for your spirit as it moves through a busy day. Write it down on a 3" x 5" card or on the appropriate page of your daybook. Look at it as often as you can. Repeat it quietly to yourself, and go on your way.

It is not meant to stop you in your tracks or to distract you from responsibilities, but simply, gently, to remind you of the presence of God and your desire to respond to this presence.

You might consider carrying with you this mantra text from the day's reading in order to let its possible meaning for you sink more deeply into your imagination. Resist the urge to pull it apart, to make clean, clear rational sense of it. A mantra is not an idea. It is a way of knowing God which emphasizes that the object of our search is immeasurably mysterious.

As Your Day Is Ending

This is a time for letting go of the day, for entering a world of imaginative prayer.

We suggest that you choose a quiet, dark place that you can

return to each day at its ending. When you come to it, your first task is to quiet your spirit. Sit, or if you are comfortable doing so, kneel. Do whatever stills your soul. Breath deeply. Inhale, exhale—slowly and deliberately, again and again until you feel your body let go of its tension.

Now, using the least possible light, follow the evening prayer slowly, phrase by phrase. Put behind you, as best you can, all that consciously or unconsciously stands between you and God.

Take as long as you need. Repeat a phrase. Repeat the whole prayer. Do whatever is comfortable, whatever stills your spirit. End when you are ready. This final prayer is an act of trust and confidence, an entryway into peaceful sleep. A simple evening prayer gathers together the spiritual character of the day that is now ending as it began—in the presence of God.

It is a time for summary and closure.

Invite God to embrace you with love and to protect you through the night.

Sleep well.

These Forty Days

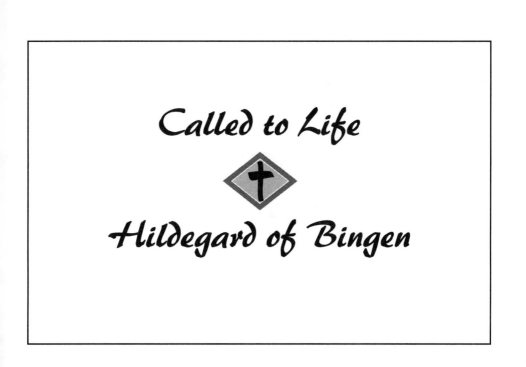

Day One

ASH WEDNESDAY

My Day Begins

We are born, each of us, with a desire for good
and a lust for evil.
We are called to life
and attracted to death.
We hear: "Do good,"
and we respond: "Choose pleasure."
Sometimes when God reaches out to us
we disdain him.

Called to Life: Hildegard of Bingen

Even so, God does not forsake us.
His gracious pity shows itself in our lives
in an abundance of mercy and compassion,
looking upon the sorrows
of all who attempt to follow him.
He is with us to console and save our souls,
to prepare us for eternal life,
not eternal death.
His grace goes before us
so that the good may not fall,
and sinners may rise again.
His grace precedes and follows us,
touches and warms us,
so that we can with passion
receive and fulfill his words of life.

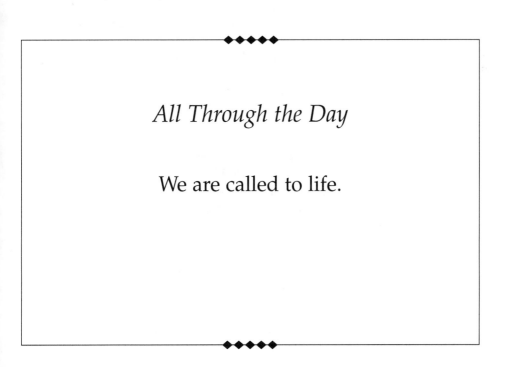

All Through the Day

We are called to life.

My Day Is Ending

In the dying of this day
help me to glimpse
the first light of a new day
and the beginnings of a new life.
Put to rest
the sorrows and failures of this day.
Let your grace go before me
into this night.
In your abundant mercy and compassion
warm me with your touch
so that in the days to come
I can eagerly receive
and passionately fulfill your words of life.

Day Two

▼

My Day Begins

We are widely different
from each other,
full of defects, stupid and blind,
impervious to the good things of the Lord,
blithely ignoring what we should praise,
preferring what we should abhor.

When we should be doing the works of justice,
we choose often as not the works of evil.

Called to Life: Hildegard of Bingen

But God our Father,
contemplating us like any father,
hugs us, his children, close to his breast.
Because he is God
he has the tender love of a father for his children.
Indeed so great is his love for us
that he sent his only Son to the cross,
like a meek lamb carried to the slaughter.
And his Son brought back the lost sheep,
bearing them on his shoulder,
precious stones and pearls
with which to grace the lump of dark clay
that he hugs to his breast.

All Through the Day

He holds our dark clay to his breast.

My Day Is Ending

In the dying of this day
help me to glimpse
the first light of a new day
and the beginnings of a new life.
Help me to understand
how great is your love for all of us,
your children.
You sent your only Son to the cross
to bring back the lost sheep,
to bring me back to where I belong,
to a new life
in the arms of your compassion.

Day Three

▼

My Day Begins

Virtue stands before us,
like a blindingly beautiful woman,
beckoning to us,
terrible as lightning,
welcome as the sun.

Her awesome beauty and her gentleness
are incomprehensible.
The godlike brilliance of her face,

the shining beauty of her garments
are blinding.
But she is within us and within everyone,
sustaining us,
turning away from no one,
not even when we resist
her every advance.
Those who follow her
are those who have chosen
to leave behind their unbelief
and their sinful choices.
They have chosen
to put on a new garment of eternal life.
To them, to us, she says:
"Do not turn back."

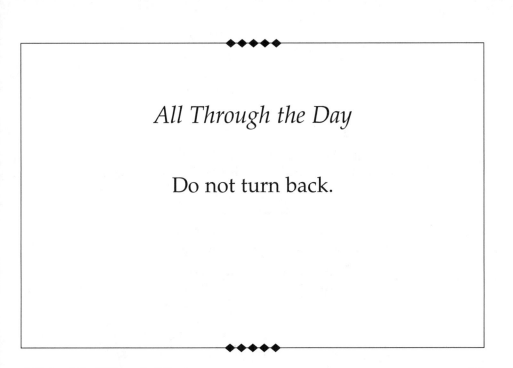

All Through the Day

Do not turn back.

My Day Is Ending

In the dying of this day
help me to glimpse
the first light of a new day
and the beginnings of a new life.
You are within me and within everyone,
sustaining us,
turning away from no one,
not even when we resist
your every advance.
Help me leave behind my unbelief,
my flirting with death.
Help me to not turn away from life.

Day Four

My Day Begins

If someone who loved you very much
gave you a great treasure
and said to you:
"Profit from this, grow rich,
but let everyone know who gave you this treasure,"
you would work very hard at
fulfilling his request.

This is what your Creator has done.
He loves you greatly,

for you are his creature,
and he has given you great treasures.
But with his gifts
comes the condition
that you apply his gifts to good works,
that you grow in virtue.
Your task then
is to make your gift valuable to others
through works of justice,
so that your life and deeds
will mirror their giver.

All Through the Day

Let your life mirror its giver.

My Day Is Ending

In the dying of this day
help me to glimpse
the first light of a new day
and the beginnings of a new life,
not just for me,
but for others.
Your gifts of love and justice
are not meant to be hoarded,
but to be multiplied,
to be passed through our lives
into the lives of everyone in reach
of our hands and our hearts,
everyone you have called to life.

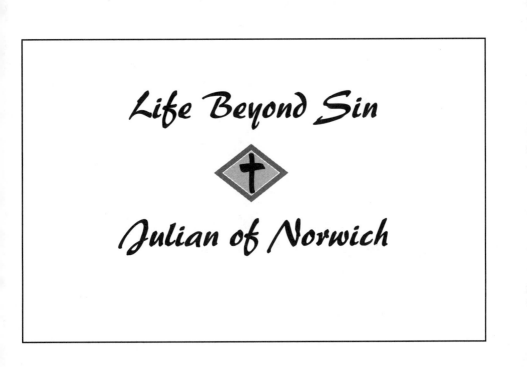

Day Five

My Day Begins

Our life in this world
consists of a wondrous mixture of good and bad.
At one moment
we are raised up,
in the next, allowed to fall.
And this fluctuation is so confusing
that we hardly know where we stand.
But what a marvelous confusion!

God wants us to trust that he is always with us.
And in the midst of our confusion

he is with us in three ways:
in heaven, where in his rising
he raises us up with him;
on earth, where he leads us day by day;
and in our innermost being,
where he constantly dwells
to guide and preserve us.
And this is our comfort,
that we know in faith
that Christ is constantly with us,
so that we never succumb
to the pain and woe,
but always hope
for another glimpse of his presence.

All Through the Day

He is constantly with us.

My Day Is Ending

In the dying of this day
help me to glimpse
the first light of a new day
and the beginnings of a new life.
Let me live in faith
that you are constantly with me,
in good times and bad,
never succumbing
to pain and woe and confusion.
Preserve in me the sight of your presence,
glimpsed dimly here,
in the silence and dark of this gathering night.

Day Six

My Day Begins

Our Lord has reminded me
that nothing stands in our way but sin,
and it is the same for all of us.
Sin may be inevitable,
but everything will turn out for the good,
and all will be well.
He did not show me sin itself,
for it has no real substance,
it is not real.

But we must not forget
the suffering and grief it causes
in all creation,
and above all the utter shame and sacrifice
he endured because of it.

But in his voice
I never heard a hint of blame,
and since we who are guilty are not blamed,
why should we in turn blame God?

Out of his tender love he consoles us, saying:
True, sin caused this pain,
but all will be well.

THAT YOU MAY HAVE LIFE

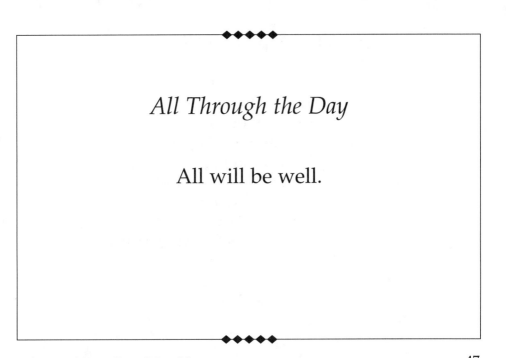

All Through the Day

All will be well.

My Day Is Ending

In the dying of this day
help me to glimpse
the first light of a new day
and the beginnings of a new life.
Remind me
of the suffering and grief
my sins have caused.
But in your voice
let me not hear the blame I have earned,
but your tender love,
telling me again
that all will be well.

Day Seven

My Day Begins

Often when we realize our faults
and our wretchedness,
we are so scared and filled with shame
that we don't know what to do.
Christ, our patient Mother,
doesn't want us to run away,
for nothing would please him less;
she wants us to behave just like a child.
When a child is terrified and frightened,

it runs to its mother as fast as it can
and calls out:
"Dear Mother, be sorry for me.
I've gotten myself into a filthy mess,
and I need your assistance and wisdom."

Even if we don't feel immediate relief,
we can be sure he is behaving as a wise Mother.
For he considers it beneficial
that we mourn and weep,
because he loves us.
He wishes us to imitate the child
who naturally trusts in its mother's love
whatever the situation.

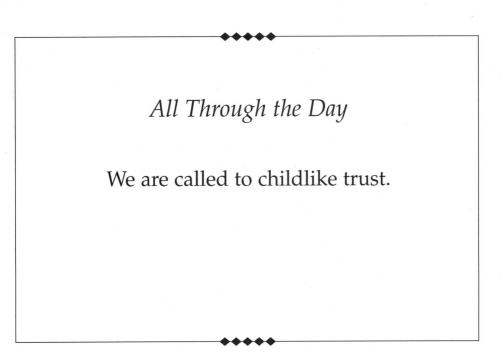

All Through the Day

We are called to childlike trust.

My Day Is Ending

In the dying of this day
help me to glimpse
the first light of a new day
and the beginnings of a new life.
You want me to imitate a child
who naturally trusts in its mother's love
whatever the situation,
no matter how frightened and filled with shame
I should be at this moment.
I won't run away from your presence.
Not now. Not tonight.
But rather I will pray for
your assistance and your wisdom.

THAT YOU MAY HAVE LIFE

Day Eight

My Day Begins

We are not called on
to endure the effects of sin by ourselves,
but are united to Jesus
in whom we behold the ground of our being.
We realize that his suffering and affliction
so far surpass anything we might endure
that we cannot fully comprehend it.
When we come to see this

we will stop weeping and lamenting
our own sufferings
and begin to understand
that though our sufferings are well deserved,
his love always excuses us.
Out of his great courtesy
he never censures us,
but instead looks upon us
with compassion and sympathy,
seeing us as righteous children without guilt.

Behold Christ's mercy upon us.

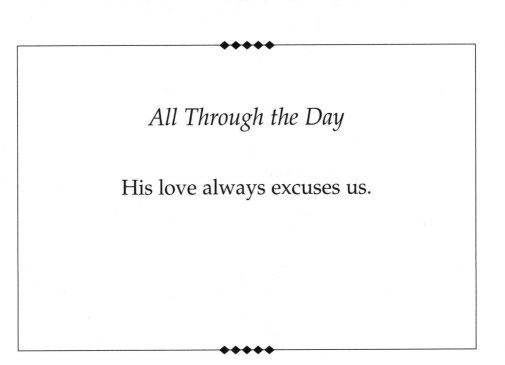

All Through the Day

His love always excuses us.

My Day Is Ending

In the dying of this day
help me to glimpse
the first light of a new day
and the beginnings of a new life.
Out of your great courtesy
do not censure me,
but instead look upon me
with compassion and sympathy.
I know that my sufferings are well deserved.
Remind me,
help me to understand,
that your love always
finds a reason to excuse me.

Day Nine

My Day Begins

Sin is the sharpest scourge
that can strike anyone's spirit.
It makes us loathsome in our own sight,
until the Holy Spirit's touch
moves us to contrition
and turns bitterness into hope in God's mercy.
The Spirit begins to heal our wounds,
revive our spirit,
and return us to life.

The Lord reaches out to us
when we seem to be almost forsaken
and cast away on account of our sin.
But because of the humility we acquire in this fashion
we are raised high in God's sight through his grace.

Contrition makes us clean,
compassion renders us ready,
and desire for God makes us worthy.

So our shame is transformed into joy and glory.
For our courteous Lord
does not wish his creatures to lose hope,
even if they fall frequently and grievously.
Our failure does not prevent him from loving us.

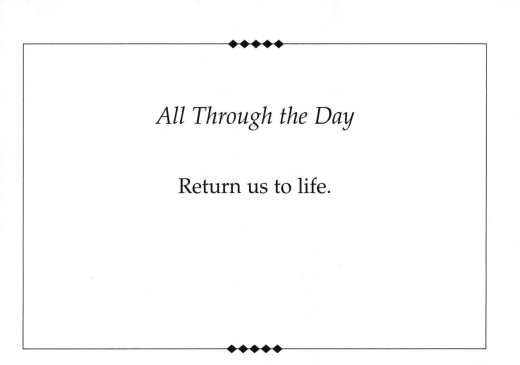

All Through the Day

Return us to life.

My Day Is Ending

In the dying of this day
help me to glimpse
the first light of a new day
and the beginnings of a new life.
Turn bitterness
into hope in your mercy.
Heal my wounds,
revive my spirit,
and return me to life.
Lord, reach out to me
when I seem to myself to be forsaken
and cast away on account of my sins.

Day Ten

My Day Begins

As long as we inhabit this impermanent life,
our good Lord,
in his merciful way,
will always lead us.
We will certainly fail
and our failure may be frightful,
our falling inglorious,
our dying wretched.

Our sin and desperation
may generate in us a wrath
and a continual opposition to peace and love.
But his mercy,
grounded in his love,
will labor within us,
preserving us
and converting everything to the good.

Never will love's compassionate eye
turn from us,
nor the operation of his mercy cease.

All Through the Day

His mercy is at work within us.

My Day Is Ending

In the dying of this day
help me to glimpse
the first light of a new day
and the beginnings of a new life.
Let me wake
to your love's compassionate eye,
your mercy
at work within me.
I know that I will certainly fail
and my failure may be frightful,
my dying wretched,
but in your mercy
preserve me.

THAT YOU MAY HAVE LIFE

Life Beyond Repentance

Meister Eckhart

Day Eleven

▼

My Day Begins

We know that
each time we repent,
love is made anew and increases.
But what is repentance?
One kind, that is earthly,
pulls us down into ever greater sorrow,
leads us to complain, and delivers us into doubt.
Such repentance is mired in misery

and goes nowhere.
Divine repentance is entirely different.
There, not content with ourselves,
we rise up at once to God,
and we turn our backs
on all sin with an adamant will.
As we rise toward God we gain certitude
and bask in a spiritual joy
that lifts us above all misery
and joins us to God.
And the weaker we are,
the more we have sinned,
the more we feel
compelled to bind ourselves to God
in pure love.

All Through the Day

Repent—and love is made new again.

My Day Is Ending

In the dying of this day
help me to glimpse
the first light of a new day,
the beginnings of a new life,
and the stirrings of repentance
in my soul.
Build on my heart's discontent;
and repentant,
my love renewed,
let me rise up at once to you,
with my back turned to all that stands
between me and your love.

Day Twelve

My Day Begins

God puts up with sin gladly,
and endures much of it.
Frequently God allows us to sin
knowing that by sinning
we will transcend our present state.
For example, who was more in love
or more intimate with our Lord than his disciples?
Yet every one of them fell into deadly sin;
every one was a mortal sinner.

Throughout the scriptures
we find that the greatest sinners
became God's truest lovers.
Even today,
you don't hear about people
accomplishing great things
without first making errors.
God wishes us
to learn from experience
the greatness of his compassion for us
so that we might be moved
toward greater humility and loyalty.

All Through the Day

The greatest sinners
can become God's truest lovers.

My Day Is Ending

In the dying of this day
help me to glimpse
the first light of a new day
and the beginnings of a new life.
I cannot come to you
as the world's greatest sinner,
nor your truest lover.
I come only as someone humbled
by a lifetime of small, persistent failures,
and small, unfilled dreams of living
loyal to you and your will,
and greatly in need of your compassion.

Day Thirteen

▼

My Day Begins

Many people think
that to show their sorrow for sin
they must do extraordinary things,
such as fasting, walking barefoot, and the like.
The best penitence, however,
is to turn away completely
from all that is not God and not divine,
whether it be in yourself
or some other person, place, or thing.

Life Beyond Repentance: Meister Eckhart

True repentance is
approaching God
in love
and squarely facing up
to what you have done.

Choose your own way of doing this,
and discover that the more you do it,
the more real your repentance will become.

True conversion
is like our Lord's passion.
The more you imitate it
the more your sins will fall away.

All Through the Day

To truly repent,
approach God in love.

My Day Is Ending

In the dying of this day
help me to glimpse
the first light of a new day
and the beginnings of a new life.
If true repentance is
approaching you in love
and squarely facing up
to what I have done,
then hear the prayers,
the truths of my heart,
that I whisper here
in the dark silence of this night,
where I am alone—and open—with you.

Day Fourteen

▼

My Day Begins

As soon as your repentance mounts up to God
your sins are swallowed up
in his compassion.

The worse you believe your sins to be,
the more ready God is
to pardon them.

God wishes to enter your soul
and drive sin out;

Life Beyond Repentance: Meister Eckhart

for no one is slow to root out
what is hateful to them.

The more there is to forgive,
the happier God is
to forgive.
And the more displeasing they are to him,
the quicker God forgives.

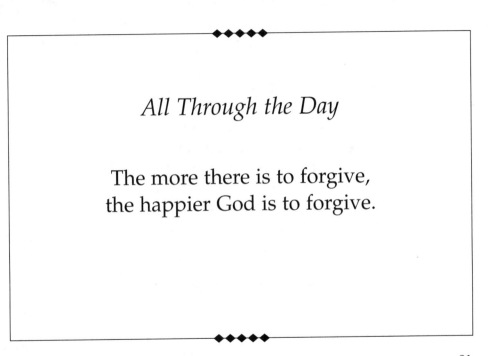

All Through the Day

The more there is to forgive,
the happier God is to forgive.

My Day Is Ending

In the dying of this day
help me to glimpse
the first light of a new day
and the beginnings of a new life.
Be quick, my Father,
to erase the sorry slate of this day,
to forgive the sins I now place
in the path of your forgiveness.
Enter my soul
and root out
everything that is hateful to you.

Day Fifteen

My Day Begins

Perfect confidence and love
cannot coexist with sin.
In fact they completely drive out sin.

Love knows nothing of sin.
Love blots it out,
and it disappears
as though it never was.
God will always choose great forgiveness
over little forgiveness.

Life Beyond Repentance: Meister Eckhart

Neither sin nor anything else
can be an obstacle to his love.
And God treats his lovers as equals
whether their sins are few or many.

For to be forgiven much
is to love much,
as our Lord Jesus pointed out,
and God's forgiveness,
like his love,
is a cup filled to the point
of running over.

All Through the Day

Confidence and love drive out sin.

My Day Is Ending

In the dying of this day
help me to glimpse
the first light of a new day
and the beginnings of a new life.
Your love can blot out sin
and make it disappear
as though it never was.
Your forgiveness,
like your love,
is a cup filled to the point
of running over.
Forgive me.

Day Sixteen

▼

My Day Begins

People sometimes
become anxious and discouraged
when they look at the lives of the saints
and realize that they are not as holy as these models,
and in truth they do not even want to be.

They jump to the conclusion
that they are cut off from God

and that they do not have what it takes
to be a disciple.
Don't ever think this way.

Nobody, at any time, is cut off from God.
No matter how imperfect you are,
or how weak.

Thinking that God is far away
can cause great damage to your soul.
For whether you are fleeing God
or returning to him,
God never leaves you.
God is always present,
always knocking at the door.

All Through the Day

Nobody at any time
is cut off from God.

My Day Is Ending

In the dying of this day
help me to glimpse
the first light of a new day
and the beginnings of a new life.
You never leave us—not one of us.
No matter how imperfect we are,
or how weak,
you are always present,
always knocking at the door.

Nobody, at any time, is cut off from you.

Not even me.

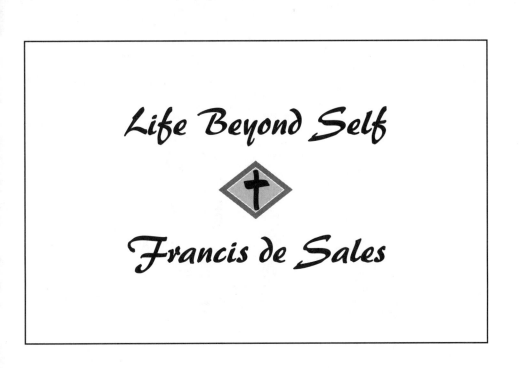

Day Seventeen

▼

My Day Begins

Nothing stands in the way
of our spiritual growth
more than self-love
and a sense of self-importance.

The moment we encounter difficulties
or something forces us to change our plans,
we are saddened and upset,
convinced that this shouldn't be happening to us,
that we need to overcome it at once.

Why?
It is because we are in love with ourselves,
with our comforts, our convenience, our good feelings.
We have come to expect that our prayers—our life—
should be steeped in orange water,
our virtues nourished by a diet of candy.
As a result we forget
Jesus prostrate on the ground,
sweating blood and water in agony,
because of the deadly conflict
in his soul.
Self-love blinds us,
makes us forget how it really is.

All Through the Day

It is self-love that stands in our way.

My Day Is Ending

In the dying of this day
help me to glimpse
the first light of a new day
and the beginnings of a new life.
But here in the dark
let me understand what it is that I pray for.
I have come to expect that my prayers—my life—
will come easily, and I forget
Jesus prostrate on the ground,
sweating blood and water in agony.
Do not let my self-love blind me
to what a new life and a new day
may bring.

Day Eighteen

▼

My Day Begins

Self-importance,
like self-love, is a disturber of our peace.

Why is it,
when we happen to commit some imperfection or sin,
that we are so surprised, upset, and impatient?
Without doubt
it is because we thought we were something special,
resolute and steady.

Therefore, when we discover that in reality
we are nothing of the kind
and have fallen flat on our face,
we are surprised and disappointed with our "self."
If we really knew ourselves well,
instead of being astonished at finding ourselves
on the ground,
we would marvel that we ever manage
to remain standing up.
In our self-importance we
expect nothing but consolation
and are caught off guard
by our weakness.

All Through the Day

It is self-importance
that disturbs our peace.

My Day Is Ending

In the dying of this day
help me to glimpse
the first light of a new day
and the beginnings of a new life
in which I will come to know myself.
Instead of being astonished at finding myself
on the ground,
let me marvel that I ever manage
to remain standing up.
In my self-importance
I expect nothing but consolation.
I should know better.
Teach me.

Day Nineteen

My Day Begins

We have to admit
that we are weak creatures,
who do hardly anything well.

It's a blow to our self-love.

We make great plans to obey God's will
and to love and serve our neighbor
in dozens of great and even heroic ways
But when it comes

to actually doing these things,
we fall short.
We come up against our humanity,
and we realize that our daily life
will never measure up to our dreams.
We will never be
as great or as perfect as we desire.

We cannot be angels,
but we can serve God
as who and what we are.

And he, in his patience,
will accept what we have to offer.

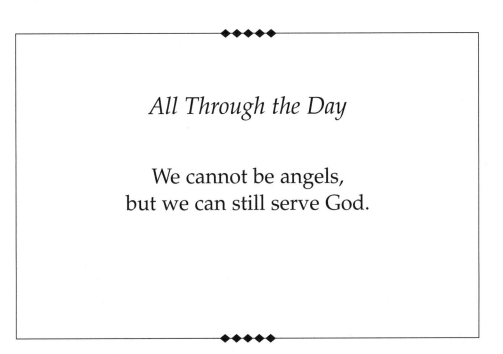

All Through the Day

We cannot be angels,
but we can still serve God.

My Day Is Ending

In the dying of this day
help me to glimpse
the first light of a new day
and the beginnings of a new life.
I have great plans for tomorrow.
I will obey your will
and love and serve my neighbor
in dozens of great and even heroic ways.
But I will fall short
and not measure up to the dreams of this silent moment.
I cannot be an angel,
but I can serve you as who and what I am.
Be patient with me—accept what I have to offer.

Day Twenty

▼

My Day Begins

It was by patient suffering
that our Lord saved us.

We can expect
to work out our salvation
in the same way:
enduring our injuries, contradictions, and annoyances
with his great calm and gentleness—
with his patience—

embracing every sort of trial
that he sends us.
Some people are willing, of course,
to suffer things that bring honor with them,
and they can be more in love
with the honor
than patient with the suffering.
But we cannot pick the trials
that improve our self-image
and avoid the ones that are merely painful.

We must bear in patience
whatever comes our way.

THAT YOU MAY HAVE LIFE

All Through the Day

We are called to bear in patience
whatever comes our way.

My Day Is Ending

In the dying of this day
help me to glimpse
the first light of a new day
and the beginnings of a new life.
It was by patient suffering
that you saved us.
Let me understand that I can expect
nothing different.
I will not be able to pick my trials,
but will have to bear in patience
whatever comes my way.
Let me borrow your patience.

Day Twenty-One

My Day Begins

The more self-conscious a spiritual life is,
the more it parades itself,
the more it desires to be seen and acclaimed,
the less likely it is
to be real and true.

True virtue and personal attractiveness
are not rooted and supported
in pride, self-sufficiency, and vanity.

Life Beyond Self: Francis de Sales

These produce a life lived
strictly for show.
It blooms brilliantly
and quickly withers away.

Having the appearance of virtue
can become very dangerous and hurtful
to those who cling to
and take delight in it.

True spirituality flowers
in humility and modesty.

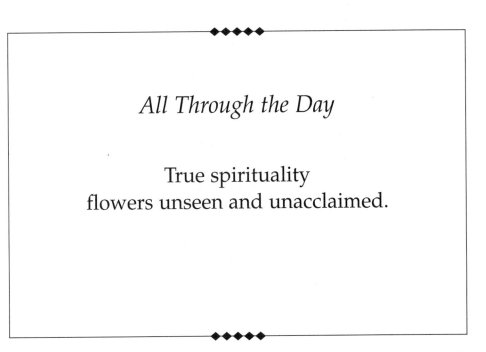

All Through the Day

True spirituality
flowers unseen and unacclaimed.

My Day Is Ending

In the dying of this day
help me to glimpse
the first light of a new day
and the beginnings of a new life.
Let the self-sufficiency that I so treasure
and have for so long sought
die with this day.
In its place
plant the seeds of humility and modesty
that alone can give strong roots
to a true spirituality.

Day Twenty-Two

▼

My Day Begins

To go beyond self
we will need
to leave behind
much that we have clung to:
the familiarity and comfort
of being self-sufficient,
our reassuring self-confidence,
our abounding self-love.

It will be painful.
As the scriptures say:
to separate us from our self-love
he will bring
"not peace but the sword."

His sword will leave our hearts raw.
We will resist with our whole being
the wrenching that precedes a fuller life.

But our peace will be found
in the midst of warfare,
our serenity will be bought
at the price of surrender.

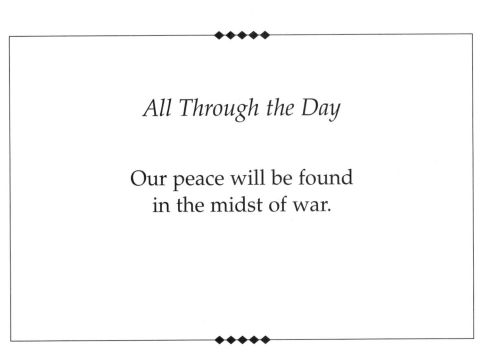

All Through the Day

Our peace will be found
in the midst of war.

My Day Is Ending

In the dying of this day
help me to glimpse
the first light of a new day
and the beginnings of a new life.
Perhaps tomorrow
I will take one small step beyond self
and leave behind
the familiarity and comfort
of being self-sufficient.
It will be painful.
You promise
"not peace but the sword."
But still I pray.
Hear me.

Day Twenty-Three

My Day Begins

Use the things of this world,
but put your trust in the things of eternity.
You cannot be fully satisfied by material possessions,
for you are simply not made to enjoy them.
Even if you owned every good thing in the world
you would not be happy and blessed,
for your blessedness and joy is in God,
who created all things.

Your happiness is not
in what is seen and admired by others,
but in what
the good and faithful followers of Christ seek.
Your happiness is in
what the spiritual and pure of heart,
those whose citizenship is in heaven,
sometimes experience in this life,
though it is meant for the next.

All Through the Day

Use the things of this world,
but put your trust in what is yet to be.

My Day Is Ending

In the dying of this day
help me to glimpse
the first light of a new day
and the beginnings of a new life
where I will no longer
put my trust,
as I did so often today,
in the things of this world.
In the light of the new day remind me
that even if I owned
every good thing in the world,
I would not be happy and blessed.
Only possessing you can do that.

Day Twenty-Four

My Day Begins

Remember the saying:
"The eyes cannot be satisfied with seeing,
nor the ears with hearing."

Strengthen me, then, Lord.
Grant that I may see beyond seeing,
hear beyond hearing,
that I may see all the things of this world
and hear all its voices

Life Beyond Things: Thomas á Kempis

as they truly are—
beyond sights, beyond sounds.
Help me to see myself in the same light,
for nothing under the sun
will last forever.
And wise is the one
who feels and understands
this to be true.
It is foolish
to seek after and put my trust
in things that perish,
to desire a long and comfortable life
and to have little care
for a good life.

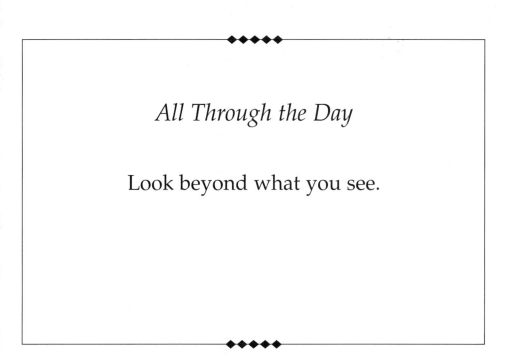

All Through the Day

Look beyond what you see.

My Day Is Ending

In the dying of this day
help me to glimpse
the first light of a new day
and the beginnings of a new life.
Grant in the light of a new day
that I may see beyond seeing,
hear beyond hearing,
see all the things of this world
and hear all its voices
as they truly are—
passing sights,
passing sounds.

Day Twenty-Five

My Day Begins

It is foolish to presume a long life
when we are not guaranteed a single day.

How many have you known
who were taken by surprise?

Death comes to everybody.
Life passes swiftly, like a shadow.
So while there is still time,
"lay up for yourself undying riches."

Life Beyond Things: Thomas á Kempis

Walk as a pilgrim and stranger on earth
for whom the things of this world
hold no final attraction.

Keep your heart free of things
and lifted up,
"for here we have no lasting city."

There will come a moment
when the poor cottage
will be more commended than the gilded palace,
when the rich of this world
will be revealed as poor.

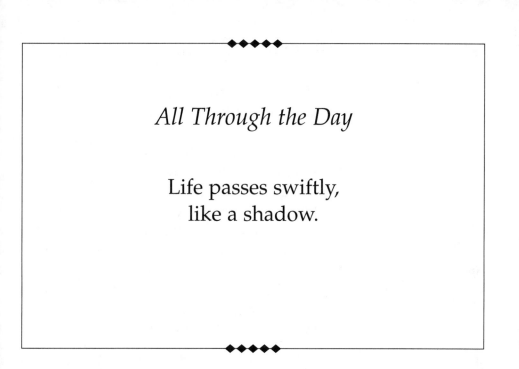

All Through the Day

Life passes swiftly,
like a shadow.

My Day Is Ending

In the dying of this day
help me to glimpse
the first light of a new day
and the beginnings of a new life.
It may not be a long life,
for you have not guaranteed us a single day.
Death comes to everybody.
Life passes swiftly, like a shadow.
So while there is time,
let me lay up undying riches,
knowing that the things of this world
have no lasting value,
that here I have no lasting city.

Day Twenty-Six

▼

My Day Begins

If you are constantly in search of this or that,
wanting to be anywhere
but where you are,
believing that you will be happier
having more or being somewhere else,
you will never know peace,
never be free of care.
In everything and every place
you will find something lacking.

Life Beyond Things: Thomas á Kempis

Adding things to your life,
multiplying them,
will not bring you peace.
Only by cutting back
and breaking their control over your life
will you find peace.

This applies not only
to money and riches,
but to the desire for honor, for praise,
and for an undemanding life.
Don't desire what you do not have.
And do not cling to anything
which stands
in the way of your freedom in God.

All Through the Day

Cling to nothing
that stands between your soul
and its freedom.

My Day Is Ending

In the dying of this day
help me to glimpse
the first light of a new day
and the beginnings of a new life.
Tomorrow I will not find more peace
than I have in all my yesterdays.
Nor will I be free of care
by adding things to my life
or by looking somewhere other than
where I am.
I will not be happier having more
or being somewhere else.
Your peace waits for me where I am.

Day Twenty-Seven

My Day Begins

When has it ever gone well for us
without God's grace?
And when has it not been well for us
when God was present?

God is our hope, our trust, our comfort,
our most faithful friend.
It is better to be poor with God
than rich without him.

So why do we continue
to place our trust
in the things of this world?

Why do we expect our consolation
to be here and now?
To trust in God, above all things,
is the only comfort
we need.

In his great goodness and generous mercy,
may he graciously
hear our prayer.

All Through the Day

It is better to be poor with God
than rich without him.

My Day Is Ending

In the dying of this day
help me to glimpse
the first light of a new day
and the beginnings of a new life.
Will I go on expecting my consolation
to be here and now,
in the things of this world,
when to trust in you above all things
is the only comfort
I need?
Enrich me
with your grace!

Day Twenty-Eight

My Day Begins

It is one thing
to reproach the world
and the things it offers us,
to recognize them as vain and treacherous.
It is quite another thing to turn our backs on them,
to resist the pull of our passions,
our vanity, our pride,
our thirst for easy comfort.

Life Beyond Things: Thomas á Kempis

But, if we must look for comfort,
we should not look for it here.
Even if we enjoy
all the comforts this world can provide,
we can be sure of one thing:
they will not last for long.

Rather, take and enjoy
what the Lord provides.
He will give us
what we need,
as much as we need,
when we need it.

All Through the Day

God will give us what we need,
as much as we need,
when we need it.

My Day Is Ending

In the dying of this day
help me to glimpse
the first light of a new day
and the beginnings of a new life.
Let me be content
to take and enjoy
what you provide,
trusting that
you will give me
what I need,
as much as I need,
when I need it.

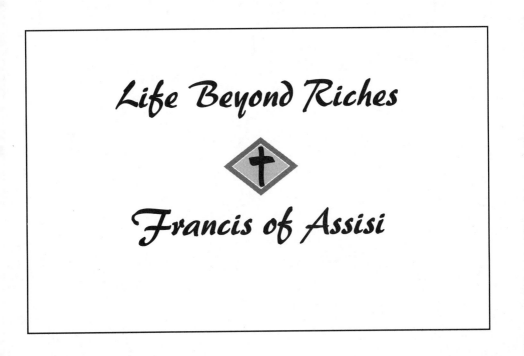

Day Twenty-Nine

My Day Begins

One day, contrary to his custom,
for he was by nature courteous,
Francis turned away from a certain poor man
who had begged alms in the name of God.

He was instantly sorry.
He told himself it was a great shame and a reproach
to withhold anything that was asked of him
in the name of so great a king.

He therefore resolved in his heart
in the future never to refuse anyone,
if at all possible,
who asked for the love of God.
This he most diligently carried out.
Long before he sacrificed himself entirely
and in every way,
he became a practitioner of the evangelical counsels.

"Give to him who begs from you," he said,
"and do not refuse him
who would borrow from you."

All Through the Day

Give what you have been given.

My Day Is Ending

In the dying of this day
help me to glimpse
the first light of a new day
and the beginnings of a new life.
Let me resolve in my heart
to give from my abundance
to those in need.
I am used to turning away
from those who beg,
clinging to what I have.
Help me to see your face in them.
You have given me everything I have.

Day Thirty

My Day Begins

One day during Mass
the gospel spoke to Francis in a special way.
Disciples of Christ, he heard the gospel say,
should not possess gold or silver or money.
As they go on their way
they should not carry scrip
or wallet or bread or staff.
They should not have shoes
or two tunics.

They should preach the kingdom of God
and repentance.

His response was immediate and joyful:
"This is meant for me.
This is what I have longed to hear.
This is how, with all my heart, I wish to live."
Immediately he began
to live out the word of the gospel.
He hurried to make part of his life
all that he had heard in the reading of the gospel.

Francis was not a passive listener to the gospel.
He took seriously what it was saying.
He committed it to memory.

All Through the Day

Act on what you hear.

My Day Is Ending

In the dying of this day
help me to glimpse
the first light of a new day
and the beginnings of a new life.
All that Francis heard in the reading of the gospel
I have heard a hundred times.
He hurried to make it part of his life.
I have acted as though it were meant
for someone else,
some other Francis, not me.
Here in the night
speak those words again.
This time I will try to listen.

Day Thirty-One

▼

My Day Begins

What others considered to be wealth,
Francis considered to be a trifle.
His ambitions were higher.
He longed to be poor with all his heart.
The world might flee and abhor poverty,
but he knew that it was treasured
by the Son of God.

Poverty became his spouse, the love of his life.
He loved her beauty,

he abandoned his father and his mother
that he might hold her more closely.
He surrendered everything else
that they might be as one.
Not for even an hour was he unfaithful to her.
This, he told his followers, was the way to perfection,
the guarantee of eternal riches.
No one desired gold as he desired poverty,
no one guarded their riches
as he guarded this jewel of the gospel.

In this way he went through life
happy, secure, and confident.
He traded the treasures of this world
for a hundredfold reward.

All Through the Day

What you consider wealth,
Francis knew was a trifle.

My Day Is Ending

In the dying of this day
help me to glimpse
the first light of a new day
and the beginnings of a new life.
Here in the dark I may honor Francis,
but in day's light I flee and abhor poverty.
I know that you treasure it,
but I am afraid to value it.
To choose poverty
would be to turn my world upside down,
to see the wealth I now value
as a trifle.
Turn this night into day.

Day Thirty-Two

My Day Begins

Francis was like a father to the poor.
On one occasion
a follower of Francis
turned on a poor man
who had asked for money:
"How do I know that you are not a rich man
pretending to be poor?"

The response deeply saddened,
even angered Francis
who rebuked the brother.
He commanded him
to strip before the poor man,
kiss his feet, and beg his pardon.
"Anyone," Francis would often say,
"who hurts the poor, hurts Christ.
The poor are an image of Christ
who made himself poor for us."

This father of the poor
made himself like the poor
in every way.

All Through the Day

Anyone who ignores the poor
ignores Christ.

My Day Is Ending

In the dying of this day
help me to glimpse
the first light of a new day
and the beginnings of a new life.
Power comes easily to me
in the presence of the powerless.
But when I hurt the poor, I hurt you.
For the poor and the powerless
are an image of you
who made yourself poor and powerless
for our sake.
Here in the dark, cut me back to size.

Day Thirty-Three

▼

My Day Begins

Bernard, a young man, first came to Francis
with a question:
"If someone has, for a long time,
been the recipient of gifts from a generous Lord
but no longer wishes to keep these gifts,
what would be the perfect thing to do?"
"Give them back," Francis replied,
"to the Lord from whom you have received them."

Early the next morning
they went together to the church.
Opening the book of gospels at random they read:
"If you would be perfect,
go, sell what you possess,
and give to the poor."

They opened the book a second time and read:
"take nothing for your journey."

And a third time:
"If any man would come after me,
let him deny himself."

Bernard did all these things.

All Through the Day

To follow Christ
is to deny self.

My Day Is Ending

In the dying of this day
help me to glimpse
the first light of a new day
and the beginnings of a new life.
Let me leave behind,
here in the dark and silence,
the possessions of a lifetime.
Prepare my soul
for a journey
on which I can take nothing.
For "if anyone would come after me,
let him deny himself."

Day Thirty-Four

My Day Begins

Who has the right words to describe
Francis' compassion for the poor?
He had, it is true, a natural kindness.
But grace doubled it.
His soul could not resist the poor,
and even when he could not give them alms
he showered them with his affection.
For when he saw someone in need,
he saw Christ.

When he came upon the nakedness of the poor,
he saw Mary's son, naked in her arms.

One day a poor and sickly man
came to where Francis was preaching.
Touched by the man's double affliction,
his poverty and his illness,
Francis spoke to his companion:
"When you see a poor man, brother,
you should see in him Christ and his mother.
It is the same when you come across a sick person.
See in him Christ
and consider the infirmities
that Christ took upon himself for our sake."

All Through the Day

Christ is everywhere you look.

My Day Is Ending

In the dying of this day
help me to glimpse
the first light of a new day
and the beginnings of a new life.
There I will see you
everywhere I look . . .
but especially in the poor,
in their powerlessness,
their need, their nakedness,
their homelessness.
Open my eyes to a new day
that I might see clearly,
for the first time.

Life Beyond Suffering

Teresa of Avila

Day Thirty-Five

▼

My Day Begins

There is no danger, my brothers and sisters,
that when you say to God,
"thy will be done,"
you will be showered
with riches or pleasures or great honors
or any earthly good.

God's love for you is not so cautious,
so halfhearted.

Life Beyond Suffering: Teresa of Avila

God places a higher value on your offer,
wishing to reward you generously,
giving you a share
in the heavenly kingdom,
even in this life.

And if you would like to see
how God treats those
who pray without reservation,
"thy will be done,"
look at Jesus.
In the garden of Gethsemane
he uttered it truthfully and resolutely.

All Through the Day

Thy will be done—
whatever it is.

My Day Is Ending

In the dying of this day
help me to glimpse
the first light of a new day
and the beginnings of a new life.
I know too well, here in the darkness,
that there is still a part of me
that wants to be showered
with riches and pleasures and honors,
that holds out the hope
that you will not take me at my word.
But thy will be done.
Whatever it is.

Day Thirty-Six

My Day Begins

You will see, my brothers and sisters,
what God gives to those he loves best.

See how the prayer of Jesus was answered—
with trials, with sufferings,
with insults and persecutions,
until at last
his life ended on the cross.

Life Beyond Suffering: Teresa of Avila

These are heaven's gifts in this world,
and God grants them
as a sign of affection for us,
to each of us
according to the courage and the love
we bear for God.

Fervent love can suffer much,
tepidity very little.
For my part,
I believe that
our love is measured
by the crosses we carry.

All Through the Day

The cross takes the measure of our love.

My Day Is Ending

In the dying of this day help me to glimpse
the first light of a new day
and the beginnings of a new life.
If our love is to be measured
by the crosses we carry,
I am afraid that you will find in me
a frightened, tepid soul capable of very little.
I am bowed down
by even the slightest burden.
Fervent love can suffer much, my tepidity very little.
You know best how heavy a cross I can carry.

Day Thirty-Seven

▼

My Day Begins

One day my Lord said to me:
"Believe me, my daughter,
trials are the heaviest for those
my father loves the best.
Trials are God's measure of love.
How could I better demonstrate
my love for you
than by desiring for you
what I desired for myself?"

Life Beyond Suffering: Teresa of Avila

It may be painful to give up pleasures,
torment to forego honor,
intolerable to bear a harsh word.
It is difficult to accept whatever suffering
comes our way,
to stop at nothing short
of dying to this world.
But this is the cost
of going where God leads us,
of following Jesus into the Garden of Gethsemane
and on to Calvary.
And only then,
to Easter morning.

All Through the Day

The garden awaits.

My Day Is Ending

In the dying of this day
help me to glimpse
the first light of a new day
and the beginnings of a new life.
There are no easy ways.
Trials are the heaviest for those
you love the best.
I know what I must say as this day ends:
"Desire for me
what you desired for your own Son."
But hear the fear in my voice.

Day Thirty-Eight

HOLY THURSDAY

My Day Begins

When we watch Jesus
on his way into the garden
this Thursday night,
we have to wonder
how great his dread must have been
to cause him,
who was patience itself,

not only to show it, but to speak of it.
Listen to him as he says:
"My soul is sorrowful unto death."
Then ask yourself:
If he admitted that his flesh was weak,
how can we expect more of our flesh?

So let us not trouble ourselves about our fears,
nor lose heart at the sight of our frailty,
but humbly remind ourselves
that without the grace of God
we are nothing.
And then, distrusting our own strength,
let us commit ourselves
to his mercy.

THAT YOU MAY HAVE LIFE

All Through the Day

Trust yourself to his mercy.

My Day Is Ending

In the dying of this day
help me to glimpse
the first light of a new day
and the beginnings of a new life.
Here in the garden
let me see what lies beyond the suffering.
Let me not be surprised by my fears,
nor lose heart at the sight of my frailty,
but humbly remind myself
that without your grace,
without your mercy,
I am nothing.

Day Thirty-Nine

▼

GOOD FRIDAY

My Day Begins

Put yourself
at the foot of the cross.
The dying Jesus has been deserted by some,
denied by others.
It is a moment of utter loneliness.

Think of his sufferings;
but more important,

think of those for whom he is enduring them,
who it is that endures them,
and the love with which he is bearing them.

Remain with him
in the silence of understanding.
Look upon him who is looking upon you
and be grateful
for where you find yourself.
There is no way
you could ever have deserved
to share this moment with him.

All Through the Day

Abundant life begins here.

My Day Is Ending

In the dying of this day
help me to glimpse
the first light of a new day
and the beginnings of a new life.
Let me see in the dark and silence of this night
the painful beginnings of new life.
You have not forsaken us,
you have not ignored our thirst,
but it is easy to think so.
If Christ could cry out
and admit the terrible emptiness of the day,
I need not be ashamed to do so.
Into your hands I commend my spirit.

Day Forty

HOLY SATURDAY

My Day Begins

As for me, given a choice,
I would always choose
the way of suffering,
not just because it allows me
to imitate the way of Jesus,
but because it brings many other blessings with it.
We cannot understand

how suffering can be a grace,
and how great a blessing it is,
until we have left all things.

For if we are attached to any one thing
it is because we set a value on it.
It may be painful
to surrender what we value,
but what greater loss,
what greater blindness,
what greater calamity could there be
than to make much
of what is nothing,
to cling to what has no value?

All Through the Day

Let go.

My Day Is Ending

In the dying of this day
help me to glimpse
the first light of a new day
and the beginnings of a new life.
The old day is dying.
The new day has yet to come.
The dark and silence of this night
is for letting go
and hoping beyond hope,
for living beyond this passing pain,
for preparing to wake
to life beyond death.

"I have come
that you might have life,
and have it more abundantly."

THAT YOU MAY HAVE LIFE

Let no one bewail their poverty;
the kingdom of heaven is opened to all.
Let no one deplore their offenses;
pardon has come from the tomb.
Let no one fear death;
the death of our savior
has freed us from the slavery of death.

He has been overcome by death
and thereby has in turn overcome it.
He has descended into hell
and rebuked it.
Death was rejected,
for it was overturned.
It took flesh and received God.

It seized earth and found heaven.
It received that which was visible
and fell into that which was invisible.

O death, where is your victory?
O death, where is your sting?
Christ has risen,
and death has been cast down.
Christ has risen,
and the devils have fallen.
Christ has risen,
and the angels rejoice.
Christ has risen,
and there are no corpses left in the sepulcher.
For Christ, in rising from the dead,

is the first fruits of those that sleep.
To him be glory and power,
forever and ever.
Amen.

Other Titles in the *Thirty Days with a Great Spiritual Teacher* series:

ALL WILL BE WELL
Based on the Classic Spirituality of *Julian of Norwich*
◆
FEAR NOT THE NIGHT
Based on the Classic Spirituality of *John of the Cross*
◆
GOD AWAITS YOU
Based on the Classic Spirituality of *Meister Eckhart*
◆
LET NOTHING DISTURB YOU
A Journey to the Center of the Soul with *Teresa of Avila*
◆
LET THERE BE LIGHT
Based on the Visionary Spirituality of *Hildegard of Bingen*
◆
LIVING IN THE PRESENCE OF GOD
The Everyday Spirituality of *Brother Lawrence*

PEACE OF HEART
Based on the Life and Teachings of *Francis of Assisi*

◆

SET ASIDE EVERY FEAR
Love and Trust in the Spirituality of *Catherine of Siena*

◆

SET YOUR HEART FREE
The Practical Spirituality of *Francis de Sales*

◆

SIMPLY SURRENDER
Based on the Little Way of *Thérèse of Lisieux*

◆

TRUE SERENITY
Based on Thomas á Kempis' *The Imitation of Christ*

◆

WHERE ONLY LOVE CAN GO
A Journey of the Soul into *The Cloud of Unknowing*

◆

YOU SHALL NOT WANT
A Spiritual Journey Based on *The Psalms*